Learning World ❶ Handwriting b

本書について
本書 Handwriting for Learning World 1は、Learning World Book 1 を使用中の子供達が、文単位（意味のかたまり）で文字に慣れることを目的としています。

テキストの音声を最初に聞くことが基本となりますが、聞くだけに留まらず、「聞きながら文字を指さす」→「聞いてから、すぐに文字をなぞる」ことによって、音声と文字のつながりを認識し、より一層「書く、読む」という活動に親しむことができるようになります。Learning World Book 1の生徒用アプリを活用して、Listeningの宿題と合わせてお使いください。

Learning World Book 1
生徒用アプリ

進度を一目でわかるために
b の表紙の下にある楕円内の数字 (6,12,18,24,…60) は Learning World 1テキスト左ページのページ番号を、下の words の楕円の数字(4,8/10,12,14…)はLearning World 1テキストのwords 欄のページを表しています。生徒が「上手になぞる」ことができたら各ページの楕円の上にシールを貼っていきます。1年後にはすべての楕円上にシールが貼られることをめざします。これにより生徒の学習進度を年間通して視覚的に把握することができます。

本書の構成
　本書はa,bの2冊からできています。「a のワーク」には各 Unit の1と3、「b のワーク」には各Unitの2とWordsをなぞって書くように構成してあります。

　2分冊にすることで、1週ごとに a, b のワークを交互に提出させることによって、レッスンの時間を割くことなく、次週のレッスンまでの間に指導者が添削の時間をもてるようにしました。

使い方（例：Unit 1の場合）

1 回目のレッスン (Unit1-1)	クラスで1-1を学習した後、「a ワーク」1-1を書く宿題として渡す。
2 回目のレッスン (Unit1-2)	生徒は宿題で練習した「a ワーク」を先生に提出。 クラスで1-2を学習した後、「b ワーク」1-2を書く宿題として渡す。
3 回目のレッスン (Unit1-3)	生徒は宿題で練習した「b ワーク」を先生に提出。 指導者は添削した「a ワーク」を生徒に返却。 クラスで1-3を学習した後、「a ワーク」1-3を書く宿題として出す。
4 回目のレッスン(Unitの復習)	生徒は宿題で練習した「a ワーク」を先生に提出。 指導者は添削した「b ワーク」を生徒に返却。 「b ワーク」Unit1のWordsを書く宿題として出す。

Listening & Writing Homework

1. 生徒用アプリの音声をかけ、何度も聞いてみよう（聞くだけでなく、真似て言うことができたらGood！）。

2. 音声を聞きながら、会話文、単語、歌などを指でさし、真似て言ってみよう。

3. 音声を聞いた後、音が耳に残っている間に文字を指でなぞってみよう。

4. 指でなぞった後に、グレーの文字を上から順になぞって書いてみよう。

JN118504

文を声に出して言いながらなぞりましょう。 Trace each sentence while saying it out loud.

My name is Jamie.

What's your name?

My name is Sara.

What's your name?

My name is Paul.

What's your name?

My name is Nancy.

What's your name?

I am Jamie.   You are Sara.

I am Sara.   You are Paul.

I am Paul.   You are Nancy.

I am Nancy. You are Jamie.

Words

1 2 3 4 5 6 7 8 9 10

one   two   three   four   five

six   seven   eight   nine   ten

12   p.8

father   mother   brother   sister

grandpa   grandma   dogs   cats

文を声に出して言いながらなぞりましょう。 Trace each sentence while saying it out loud.

This is China. Let's say "Ni hao."

This is America. Let's say "Hello."

This is Kenya. Let's say "Jambo."

This is Germany.

Let's say "Guten Tag."

This is Thailand.

Let's say "Sawasdee Ka."

This is Japan.

Let's say "Konnichiwa."

Words

Date /

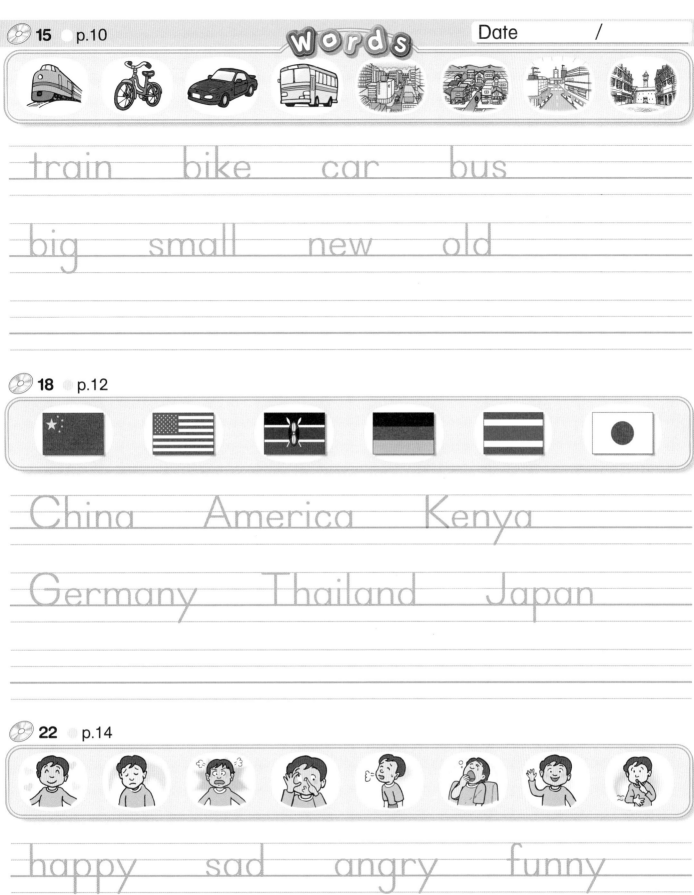

train bike car bus

big small new old

China America Kenya

Germany Thailand Japan

happy sad angry funny

tired sleepy fine hungry

文を声に出して言いながらなぞりましょう。 Trace each sentence while saying it out loud.

How is the weather?

It's rainy.

Let's play video games.

OK.

♪ 30 p.19

Rain, rain, go away

Come again another day

Little Jamie wants to play

Rain, rain, go away

Words

Date /

hair   face   neck   arms   belly

legs   feet   hands   teeth

rainy   sunny   cloudy   windy

snowy   hot   cold

go   run   walk   sing   dance

shout   stop   eat   drink   cook

文を声に出して言いながらなぞりましょう。 Trace each sentence while saying it out loud.

Look at the pumpkins! Big fat pumpkins!

Look at the grapes! Juicy purple grapes!

Look at the rice! Shiny white rice!

Thank you, Sun.

Thank you, Rain.

Thank you, beautiful EARTH!

words

11 12 13 14 15 16 17 18 19 20

eleven   twelve   thirteen   fourteen

fifteen   sixteen   seventeen

eighteen   nineteen   twenty

40 ● p.24

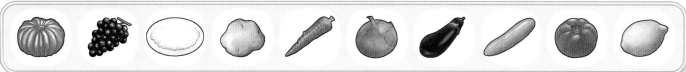

pumpkin   grapes   rice   potato

carrot   onion   eggplant   cucumber

tomato   lemon

43 ● p.26

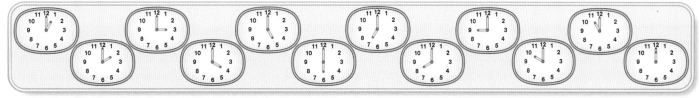

one o'clock   two o'clock   three o'clock

four o'clock   five o'clock   six o'clock

seven o'clock   eight o'clock   nine o'clock

ten o'clock   eleven o'clock   twelve o'clock

ぶん　こえ　だ　　い
文を声に出して言いながらなぞりましょう。　Trace each sentence while saying it out loud.

I like my pet.

A big black duck.

It's big.　It's black.

I have a pet.　A big black duck!

I like my pet.

A little purple turtle.

It's little.　It's purple.

I have a pet.　A little purple turtle!

Words

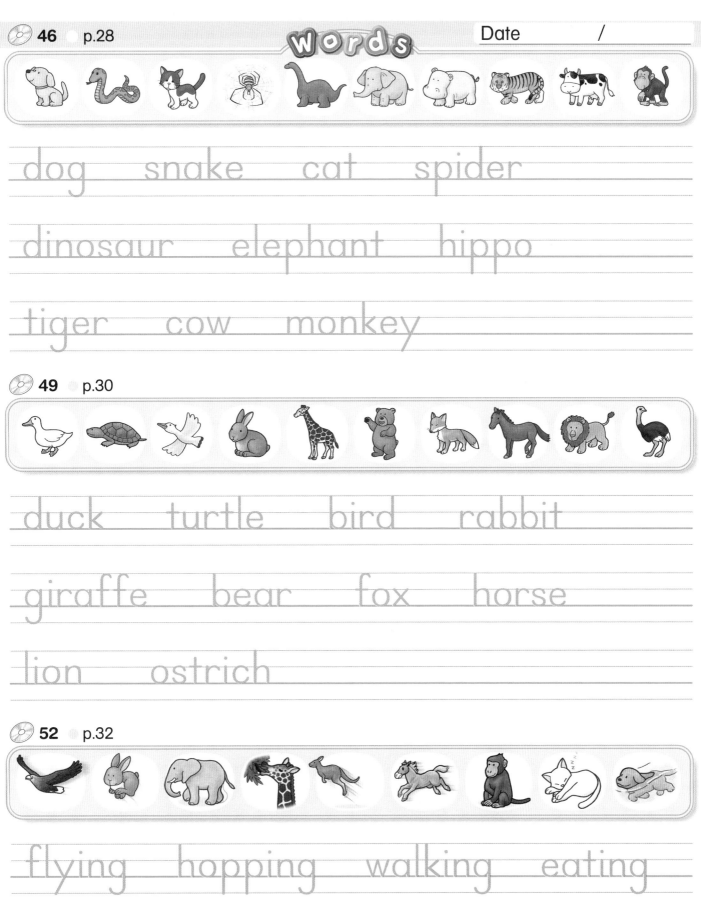

dog   snake   cat   spider

dinosaur   elephant   hippo

tiger   cow   monkey

49 ● p.30

duck   turtle   bird   rabbit

giraffe   bear   fox   horse

lion   ostrich

52 ● p.32

flying   hopping   walking   eating

jumping   running   sitting

sleeping   swimming

文を声に出して言いながらなぞりましょう。 Trace each sentence while saying it out loud.

Let's eat dinner.　Yum yum yum.

Wash your hands and set the table.

Get your forks and get your knives.

Salt, pepper, glasses and plates.

Let's eat dinner.　Yum yum yum.

Words

pancakes   spaghetti   salad   cereal

cake   ice cream   fried chicken

pizza   apple pie   cheese

table   fork   knife   salt   pepper

glass   plate   spoon   milk

orange juice

big/little   short/long   new/old

clean/dirty   left/right   up/down

文を声に出して言いながらなぞりましょう。   Trace each sentence while saying it out loud.

What's he wearing today?

What color is his shirt?

What color is his cap?

What color are his pants?

What's he wearing today?

Words

Date   /

sweater   cap   blouse   shorts

dress   socks   sneakers

67   p.42

shirt   pants   skirt   shoes

hat   belt

70   p.44

pretty   nice   good   cute   cool

new   clean   beautiful

文を声に出して言いながらなぞりましょう。　Trace each sentence while saying it out loud.

Can you swim?　Yes, I can.

Can you swim?　Yes, I can.

Can you ski?　No, I can't.

Can you ski?　No, I can't.

Can you skate?　Yes, I can.

Can you skate?　Yes, I can.

Words

Date /

teacher   singer   actress   actor

baseball player   soccer player

scientist   doctor

swim   ski   skate   read   write

draw   climb   drive a car

文を声に出して言いながらなぞりましょう。 Trace each sentence while saying it out loud.

 I'm one year old.

 I'm ten years old.

 I'm twenty years old.

 I'm thirty years old.

 I'm forty years old.

 I'm fifty years old.

 I'm sixty years old.

 I'm seventy years old.

 I'm eighty years old.

 I'm ninety years old.

 I'm one hundred years old.

Unit 9-1 84/85 p.52 ⇨ Handwriting b **p.21**

88 p.54

| 1 | 10 | 20 | 30 | 40 | 50 | 60 | 70 | 80 | 90 | 100 |

one   ten   twenty   thirty   forty

fifty   sixty   seventy   eighty

ninety   one hundred

91 p.56

book   eraser   bag   shoe   pencil

ruler   textbook   notebook   stapler

pencil case

文を声に出して言いながらなぞりましょう。 Trace each sentence while saying it out loud.

 What is your favorite animal?

 I like lions.

 What is your favorite fruit?

 I like grapefruits.

 What is your favorite color?

 I like yellow.

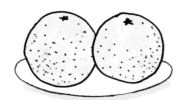

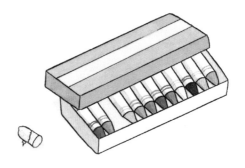

Words

get up   go to school   go home

take a bath   go to bed

Unit 9-1 84/85   p.52

Words

January   February   March

April   May   June   July   August

September   October   November

December

Sunday   Monday   Tuesday

Wednesday   Thursday   Friday

Saturday

Date   /

I Have a Joy

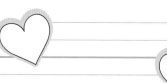

I have a joy, joy, joy, joy,

down in my heart,

down in my heart,

down in my heart,

I have a joy, joy, joy, joy,

down in my heart,

down in my heart to stay!

Skidamarink a doo

Skidamarink a dink a dink,

Skidamarink a doo, I love you.

Skidamarink a dink a dink,

Skidamarink a doo, I love you.

I love you in the morning

and in the afternoon.

I love you in the evening

and underneath the moon.

Oh, skidamarink a dink a dink,

Skidamarink a doo, I love you.

Learning World ❶
Handwriting ɑ

本書について

本書 Handwriting for Learning World 1は、Learning World Book 1 を使用中の子供達が、文単位（意味のかたまり）で文字に慣れることを目的としています。

テキストの音声を最初に聞くことが基本となりますが、聞くだけに留まらず、「聞きながら文字を指さす」→「聞いてから、すぐに文字をなぞる」ことによって、音声と文字のつながりを認識し、より一層「書く、読む」という活動に親しむことができるようになります。Learning World Book 1の生徒用アプリを活用して、Listeningの宿題と合わせてお使いください。

Learning World Book 1
生徒用アプリ

進度を一目でわかるために

ɑ の表紙の下にある楕円内の偶数の数字（4,8,10,14,…,62）は Learning World 1テキスト左ページのページ番号を表しています。生徒が「上手になぞる」ことができたら各ページの楕円の上にシールを貼っていきます。1年後にはすべての楕円上にシールが貼られることをめざします。これにより生徒の学習進度を年間通して視覚的に把握することができます。

本書の構成

本書はɑ, bの2冊からできています。「ɑ のワーク」には各 Unit の1と3、「bのワーク」には各Unitの2とWordsをなぞって書くように構成してあります。

2分冊にすることで、1週ごとに ɑ, b のワークを交互に提出させることによって、レッスンの時間を割くことなく、次週のレッスンまでの間に指導者が添削の時間をもてるようにしました。

使い方（例：Unit 1の場合）

1回目のレッスン (Unit1-1)	クラスで1-1を学習した後、「ɑ ワーク」1-1を書く宿題として渡す。
2回目のレッスン (Unit1-2)	生徒は宿題で練習した「ɑ ワーク」を先生に提出。 クラスで1-2を学習した後、「bワーク」1-2を書く宿題として渡す。
3回目のレッスン (Unit1-3)	生徒は宿題で練習した「b ワーク」を先生に提出。 指導者は添削した「ɑ ワーク」を生徒に返却。 クラスで1-3を学習した後、「ɑ ワーク」1-3を書く宿題として出す。
4回目のレッスン(Unitの復習)	生徒は宿題で練習した「ɑ ワーク」を先生に提出。 指導者は添削した「bワーク」を生徒に返却。 「bワーク」Unit1のWordsを書く宿題として出す。

Listening & Writing Homework

1. 生徒用アプリの音声をかけ、何度も聞いてみよう（聞くだけでなく、真似て言うことができたら Good!）。

2. 音声を聞きながら、会話文、単語、歌などを指でさし、真似て言ってみよう。

3. 音声を聞いた後、音が耳に残っている間に文字を指でなぞってみよう。

4. 指でなぞった後に、グレーの文字を上から順になぞって書いてみよう。

文を声に出して言いながらなぞりましょう。 Trace each sentence while saying it out loud.

 Hello. My name is Jamie.

What's your name?

 My name is Sara.

Nice to meet you.

Nice to meet you, too.

How old are you, Sara?

I'm seven years old.

How old are you?

I'm seven years old, too.

ぶん こえ だ い
文を声に出して言いながらなぞりましょう。 Trace each sentence while saying it out loud.

Who's she?

She's my mother.

What's her name?

Her name is Nancy.

Who's he?

He's my father.

What's his name?

His name is Paul.

3

文を声に出して言いながらなぞりましょう。 Trace each sentence while saying it out loud.

Where do you live?

I live in Yokohama.

Yokohama is a big city.

How do you come to school?

I come to school by train.

4

文を声に出して言いながらなぞりましょう。 Trace each sentence while saying it out loud.

Let's make a face.

A happy happy face.

Eyes, a nose, and a mouth.

Let's make a face. A sad sad face.

Eyes, a nose, and a mouth.

Let's make a face.

An angry angry face.

Eyes, a nose, and a mouth.

Let's make a face.

A funny funny face.

Eyes, a nose, and a mouth.

ぶん こえ だ い
文を声に出して言いながらなぞりましょう。 Trace each sentence while saying it out loud.

Wash, wash, wash. Wash yourself clean.

Hair, hair, hair. Wash your hair clean.

Face, face, face. Wash your face clean.

Neck, neck, neck. Wash your neck clean.

Arms, arms, arms. Wash your arms clean.

Belly, belly, belly. Wash your belly clean.

Legs, legs, legs. Wash your legs clean.

Feet, feet, feet. Wash your feet clean.

Wash, wash, wash. Wash yourself clean.

ぶん こえ だ い
文を声に出して言いながらなぞりましょう。 Trace each sentence while saying it out loud.

Go. Let's go.

Run. Let's run.

Walk. Let's walk.

Sing. Let's sing.

Dance. Let's dance.

Shout. Let's shout.

Stop. Let's stop.

7

ぶん こえ だ い
文を声に出して言いながらなぞりましょう。 Trace each sentence while saying it out loud.

How many coins do I have?

One, two, three, four, five.

Five coins!

How many coins do I have?

One, two, three, four, five, six, seven,

eight, nine, ten, eleven.

Eleven coins.

How many coins do I have?

One, two, three, four, five, six, seven,

eight, nine, ten, eleven, twelve,

thirteen, fourteen,

fifteen. Fifteen coins!

8

文を声に出して言いながらなぞりましょう。 Trace each sentence while saying it out loud.

What time?   What time?

What time is it?

It's three o'clock!

What time?   What time?

What time is it?

It's ten o'clock!

文を声に出して言いながらなぞりましょう。　Trace each sentence while saying it out loud.

Do you like dogs?

Yes, I do. Yes, I do.

I like dogs.

Do you like snakes?

No, I don't. No, I don't.

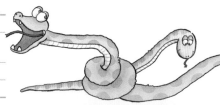

I don't like snakes.

Do you like cats?

Yes, I do. Yes, I do.

I like cats.

Do you like spiders?

No, I don't. No, I don't.

I don't like spiders.

10

文を声に出して言いながらなぞりましょう。   Trace each sentence while saying it out loud.

Look!

A bird is flying.

Look!

A rabbit is hopping.

Look!

An elephant is walking.

Look!

A giraffe is eating a leaf.

文を声に出して言いながらなぞりましょう。 Trace each sentence while saying it out loud.

 I'm hungry.

 Do you want some pancakes?

 Yes, I do.

 Here you are.

 Thank you, Mom.

文を声に出して言いながらなぞりましょう。 Trace each sentence while saying it out loud.

When I say big, we say little.

When I say short, we say long.

I have a big bag.

We have a little bag.

I have a short pencil.

We have a long pencil.

Big, little, short, long,

big, little, short, long!

文を声に出して言いながらなぞりましょう。   Trace each sentence while saying it out loud.

 Whose sweater is this?

 It's my sweater.

 Is this your cap?

 No, it isn't.

It's Sara's cap.

文を声に出して言いながらなぞりましょう。　Trace each sentence while saying it out loud.

 I like your shirt.

It's pretty.

 Thank you, Jamie.

I like your pants.

They are nice.

 Thank you, Sara.

文を声に出して言いながらなぞりましょう。 Trace each sentence while saying it out loud.

 Do you know that man?

 Yes, I do.

He is Mr. Smith.

He is our English teacher.

🎵 75 ● p.47

Do you know this man,

this man, this man?

Oh, do you know this man?

Oh, yes we do.

文を声に出して言いながらなぞりましょう。 Trace each sentence while saying it out loud.

 May I have your name, please?

 Jamie.

 How do you spell it?

 J, A, M, I, E, Jamie.

 J, A, M, I, E, Jamie.

Thank you.

81 p.51

There was a farmer had a dog,

and Bingo was his name, oh,

B-I-N-G-O, B-I-N-G-O, B-I-N-G-O,

and Bingo was his name, oh!

17

文を声に出して言いながらなぞりましょう。 Trace each sentence while saying it out loud.

 What is the date today?

 It's January 9th.

 What day is it today?

 It's Monday.

January

Sunday	Monday	Tuesday	Wednesday	Thursday	Friday	Saturday
1	2	3	4	5	6	7
8	9	10	11	12	13	14
15	16	17	18	19	20	21
22	23	24	25	26	27	28
29	30	31				

Date　　　　　　/

文を声に出して言いながらなぞりましょう。 Trace each sentence while saying it out loud.

This is mine, not yours.

It's my book.

This is mine, not yours.

It's my eraser.

This is mine, not yours.

It's my bag.

This is mine, not yours.

It's my shoe.

文を声に出して言いながらなぞりましょう。 Trace each sentence while saying it out loud.

What time do you get up?

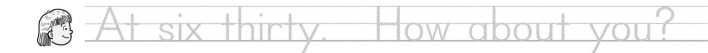

At six thirty.　How about you?

At seven o'clock.

What time do you go to bed?

At eight thirty.　How about you?

At nine o'clock.

文を声に出して言いながらなぞりましょう。 Trace each sentence while saying it out loud.

Hello.

My name is Jamie.

I am seven years old.

I live in Yokohama.

I like dogs.

I don't like snakes.

I can swim.

I can't ski.

My friend's name is Sara.

ABC Echo Song

a b c d e f g, a b c d e f g,

h i j k l m n, h i j k l m n,

o p q r s t u, o p q r s t u,

v w x y z, v w x y z.

Head, Shoulders, Knees and Toes

Head, shoulders, knees and toes,

knees and toes.

Head, shoulders, knees and toes,

knees and toes and

eyes and ears and mouth and nose,

oh, head, shoulders, knees and toes,

knees and toes.